Boulevard of Broken Dreams

POEMS BY
KATHERINE THERESE CECILIA EATMON
2017-2019

ISBN: 9780359862610
Raleigh, North Carolina
US

For my awesome children,
who I love with my whole being:
Oscar and Rachel

In memory of my sister,
Monica Therese Vermeulen Benziger
July 9, 1957-January 25, 2017

i carry your heart with me(i carry it in
my heart)i am never without it(anywhere
i go you go,my dear;and whatever is done
by only me is your doing,my darling)
i fear
no fate(for you are my fate,my sweet)i want
no world(for beautiful you are my world,my true)
and it's you are whatever a moon has always meant
and whatever a sun will always sing is you

here is the deepest secret nobody knows
(here is the root of the root and the bud of the bud
and the sky of the sky of a tree called life;which grows
higher than soul can hope or mind can hide)
and this is the wonder that's keeping the stars apart

i carry your heart(i carry it in my heart)

ee cummings

Also by Katherine T. Eatmon

Peripheral Vision: Life on the Edge of Death (2009)
Right Here: Living an Ordinary Life (2011)
Blessings: Pursuing a Spiritual Life (2012)
Traumas: The Early Poems (2014)
Camera Roll (2014)
The Clouds Will Lift (2016)

Poems

Am I gonna die?"

I can't sleep,
Lying awake in the murky dark
I hear her in my mind.
"Am I gonna die?
Fifty pounds lighter
She was swollen and hurting
As she had been for months.
"Am I gonna die?"

They gave her morphine
For her excruciating pain
And at long last she smiled.
But she faded quickly
Over the next five hours.

"Am I gonna die?"
"Yes but you are not alone."
We held her
And soon she fluttered
Like a butterfly
Then drifted away.

I dreamt about her last night.
She answered my call
"Hello?"
But in the morning
The line was dead.

"Am I gonna die?"

Gethsemane

I shrouded myself
In lilac and grape tapestries
Even before she died
She was first
Struck down
Crucified
My fading hazel eyes
Gaze toward
Suns and stars.
Delicate designs.
A purple shrine.

I protect myself
Prepare,
Anoint myself
Calm
With indigo balm
Despair
Alone in the garden.

Waiting.

November 11, 2017

Panda

> "Female giant pandas are solitary creatures except when raising their young."

Rolling from side to side
I wake slowly.
Flaking sliver trees,
Dense as a bamboo forest,
Variegate the light
Slicing through my window.
I rotate again
Then stretch my new knee.

My offspring long gone
I have become a solitary creature
Crepuscular in my habits,
Wary of daylight.
Vulnerable.

When will I be able to forage again
Go back to roaming through my days
Close to the ground?
When will I amble along
Leaving my mark on something or
Someone?

But reclusive souls do not grow lonely.
It is no longer my nature.

Arctic Dreams

The sky bursts into brilliant curtains
Of dazzling color.
I am propelled into eternal night
Beneath the pulsing pinks and greens.
This cycle has not yet wavered,
Has not shifted into abysmal days
As in the past.
The best it gets is barely twilight.

I find comfort in this dusk.
A cold and cranky arctic wind
Moves through me night after polar night.
I prowl like a bear
Stranded on the melting, muddy tundra
Desperate for the freeze-up
That forewarns winter.

With frigid fingertips
I trace the fragile blue glacial rivulets
That trickle through my wrists.

This is no climate change.
This has been my weather
Throughout my life;
Long endless nights
Under a motionless north star
Waiting for the ice floes to return.

Cross Country

For Susan

1. We couldn't have been
More different.
Yet we had forged a fragile friendship.
Your staggering sable hair
Smelled of inland canals and Canadian waterfalls.
It was December
But you were still tanned from a summer
Spent sailing on Lake Ontario.
I smelled of binding glue, reefer and Colt 45,
Proletarian gear,
From two seasons in a sweat shop.
You were optimistic, I was ornery.

We were adolescents
Young, and impulsive.
So during the worst Buffalo winter
We wandered west in your pumpkin tinged Datsun.

2. Decades later I recall
Great freshwater lakes
Steep sleepy sand dunes
Sculpted rainbow canyons
And the powerful, whispering Pacific.

Cross country,
You stride through the zealous snow
Protected by four Great Lakes.
I plod on the rolling clay hills of the Piedmont
At the foot of Blue Mountains.

Once I dreamed of enormous expanses of sea and sky,
But now my dreams are paltry;
Colorful tapestries teasing my walls,
French vanilla iced coffee close by,
New purple sheets and
Azure parakeets singing me to sleep.

Four

What is it like to lose a sister?
We were four.
The four sisters.
The little women.
Jo, Beth, Amy and Meg.
We were the four girls
Meant to be
Four always.

But, we were four and now we are three.

I see the number 4 everywhere
Four seasons
Four quarters
Four gospels
Four cardinal directions
Four elements
Four virtues...

What if there were only three?
How would that look?
What season are we willing to lose?
What virtue?

Not so easy, is it?

So we go on as three
Missing a vital part,
A gospel,
Direction...

We were four
Now we are three.
A troubled triangle

Euphausia Superba*

To avoid predators, krill feed at shallow depths during the night, diving to safer, greater depths during the day.

I flounder underwater
In this frozen southern sea
Sluggishly skimming the belly
Of ancient glaciers for slimy algae.
Pinkish swarms of simple krill
Translucent and tireless
Surround me.
We spar languidly for fodder as
Surging shadows of ultramarine icebergs
Bloat massively overhead.

A shy subtle aqua glow grows.

And I fear
A starving polar whale
Threatening the busy horde.
I break free,
Sink down down down
To the vibrant seabed.

Some of the lucky ones have followed me
To the ocean floor
If I am lucky
I will survive five, six more years of vertical migration.
We crowd together in obscurity, trembling
Amongst the subdued rainbows of pulsing
Sea feathers, stars and squirts
We doze till sunset

* Superb display (from the Greek and Latin)

Chrysalis

Most of the butterflies lived
Peeling out of their golden cocoons
Damp with birth.
Most of the painted ladies
Beat the odds
Flapping their wings
Joyfully
Like colorful quilts on a windy clothesline

The astonished children watched them sip fruit juice
Grow and thrive
And when it was time
I opened the shutters
And let them flutter away.

But a few
Trapped in stale sepia shells
Lingered shriveling on the habitat floor.

The little one who noticed
Raised her profound cocoa eyes
Pleading in anguish
"Please don't throw them in the trash!"

So I didn't.

July 23, 2018

Caregiver

When we meet
you moan resentfully
About your weak feeble mother;
your dread upon rising each morning
To the task of "cleaning her up."
But you said it crudely
Cruelly
Scrupulously watching my face
For sympathy.
You feel so burdened.

Yet I felt embarrassed for your mom
Every wakening
Lying in wait
For your stingy bit of sunrise comfort
Your bitter easing of her nightly dank distress
No matter how dismal it may seem
To you.

I wonder if you realize the blessing of
those sparkling gems of moments,
The intimacy of caregiving
And the pleasure it reaps
Upon your elderly ailing mother

However dreadful it gets
It won't last long
(Sadly to your extreme relief)
But it will end
Leaving in its place
The forever empty bed of loss

July 26, 2018

Boulevard of Broken Dreams

> "My shadow's the only one that walks beside me
> My shallow heart's the only thing that's beating
> Sometimes I wish someone out there will find me
> Till then I walk alone."

I noticed today that
There is a song on my mind
When I waken each day.
It shadows me through the hours
A steady undertow of relentless beats.

I often wonder how it goes for you,
Does lovely music follow you
On lofty clouds above?

I remember as a teen
Peeking into your room
To find you bouncing on your bed
Singing to your favorite songs
Animated like a fiery maestro in concert.

What happened to the boom box I bought you?
It haunts me.
It wasn't with your things when you died.
Had you lost your way already?
Did it shatter like an antique album
Tossed angrily to the boulevard below?

It bothers me
That you lost your lyrics
Those last few months
As you drowned in the crashing waves
Of your crafty illness.
I fear you walk alone.

August 21, 2018

Florence

For Oscar Jr.

I forecasted a category 4 disaster
which crept towards me
over several endless days
then
everything happened at once
the furious winds
the violent storms
the flash surges of images
our wedding eighteen years ago

I took the day off
donned a decent dress
but no fading flowers, no quizzical guests
just you, me and my feeble doubts

it was in that stillness
in the courtroom
in the sudden blinding light
that I perilously said "I do"

soon after
we passed through the eye wall
into the destruction that became our life

it has been raining for five days
five days of toppled trees
flooded towns
useless deaths

as the hurricane fades
into relentless torrents
of irreversible wreckage
this vague anxiety
becomes a depression
with its continued assault
of pointless memories

Sept. 15, 2018

In The Shallows

For my baby blue eyes

Fragile sand sucked at my sunken toes
As we stepped through the shallows.
Translucent triflings slid around our calves
Like zealous anklets.

We waded on Oak Island,
our silent words numerous as the stars
That began to appear
while the fish went to bed.

Strolling to the dry sand
We waited for that fortuitous moment
The International Space Station would appear,
That instant,
Timeless
As our tiny lives.

“There it is!”
Emerging from the dusky southern sky
just as you anticipated,
Hundreds of thousands of miles above.
Surely it watched us back
On its drift toward sunrise.

Gratified, we trudged up the sloping shore
The beach shifting beneath us,
You too old to hold my hand,
Me reluctant to let go.

October 18, 2018

The Dancer

> "Keep a fire burning in your eye, pay attention to the open sky
> You never know what will be coming down." Jackson Browne

We never know when to expect you
You flit in gracefully
Like a crisp autumn apple-scented day
amber leaves trailing behind.

stunned for a second,
we gaze in awe at your poise
listening to the melody in your gentle voice.

the way you teach
tenderly leads us in improvisation
a butterfly finding nectar
in a late fall flower
a ginger cat circling under a comfy cover

your hands aligned in purposeful strokes
direct our delightful dance
perfect to the final curtain call.

For Pamela
Nov. 14, 2018

Autumn

> "Still, when I think of the road
> we're traveling on
> I wonder what went wrong
> I can't help it, I wonder what went wrong"   Paul Simon

It's been a pitiful Autumn.
Endless days of rain
Warm days, cold days, in between days.
There has been no rhyme nor reason.
Now the leaves dangle like dirty socks
Dying without vibrance.

Driving this morning
I noted feeble fringes of pink
Across the dismal dawn.
Abruptly
I remembered
I dreamed of my dead husband.
He was tall and broad
Holding me in strong sweatered arms.
His smiling face was dark as almonds.
I knew I was dreaming
Regardless
I buried my face
Against his warm familiar heartbeat.

During the day,
I hear a major winter storm is on its way.
Discarded pieces of clothing litter my apartment
In musty raked piles
Fickle weather
Foul laundry
Fading leaves and
Departed loved ones
Flutter around me

As the season flees.

December 8, 2018

Snowed In

the sun rises right outside
my bedroom window.
I can watch the day begin
first
a glaze
then
a glimmer
then
glinting rays of bursting light
blinding me.
morning slices determinedly through
strips of tall pines.
when I close my eyes
I see green clouds
in a red Violet sky.

I imagine dying is like this
creeping up slowly
then brilliantly overtaking me.
will I explode into heaven glowing like a star
or
will I wane cautiously with the sunset
holding my sisters' hands ,
sightlessly finding my way?

the sun lifts above my sash
now
and I am in its afterglow.
My pup has snuck under my covers
falling asleep in the crook of my knees.
I feel his warm breathing
against my nighttime fleece.
we are both reluctant to get up.

December 11, 2018

Joshua Tree

"It's the Joshua tree's struggle that gives it its beauty."
The Glass Castle

Vandals are destroying Joshua Trees
In the Mohave Desert.
They slaughter the ugly, twisted branches
Leaving them ravaged in the relentless sun.

Last night
I dreamed I was a med student
Delivering disabled babies.
You were in the dream,
I said, "See, it's not so bad
To be born with Cerebral Palsy."
I woke and couldn't remember
Where you are.
Then I did.

It is that time of year again
Your time. Your day
Two years ago.

You had seemed to rally
The cancer was gone he said.
The doctor scrawled your next appointment
And hugged you.
I pushed your waning body
To the waiting van.
It was a mild day but
Did not feel like victory.

You were cut down by sepsis.
As we huddled around your damaged body
Weeping and praying.
You died, like those murdered yuccas
You fought beautifully, like the Joshua tree
And you became great

Like the Joshua tree.

1/14/2019

Oil Change

it's so cold
my fingers feel like icicles
as they scoop the refuse
out my car
so much trash
in such a small space
four garbage bags

finally I am done
and my nasty hands
drive to the service station

a tiny chestnut boy plays "I Spy"
I feel my anxiety pounding
and wonder if he spies my distress

I wish I could drain my feelings
replacing them with clean fresh ones
and move through life
well-oiled and renewed

my emotions remain frozen in place
like the chilly air around me
car finished I drive off
unchanged

3/6/2018

Like a Prayer

The congestion becomes severe
On our way back home.
It is irritating as
My son’s surly mood.
But soon we hear sirens and we pass
A considerable crash
With two fires engines
Three police cars
Two ambulances.
I do a quick sign of the cross
Then silently like a prayer
“God please help those people.”

I drop grumpy off at home
And go on an errand.
Back, I park and listen to the radio.
Madonna, Cyndi Lauper…
Then silently
Like a prayer
“God please help me”
Before I return to
The wreck that is my life.

April 14, 2019

Black Hole

Scientists from eight places around the world
Spent years planning
To take a photo of the elusive black hole.
After seven synchronized days
The thousand pounds of data was collected
And flown to Arizona.

And there it was,
An image of the unobservable,
A cosmic abyss so deep and dense
That not even light can escape it.

I have not eaten today.
I could say I didn't want to tear myself away
From listening to Fleetwood Mac,
Or from reading Ordinary People,
Or watching funny dog videos on YouTube.
But I don't think any of those
Apply.

I enjoy this gnawing
In my stomach.
Distracting me from the supernova
Inside me.
I don't need a visual of my great void to see
Effigies of aneurysms, cancer,
Deathbeds and abandonment.

I don't need to collaborate or prepare for
The sudden shock of thundering flashbacks
Throbbing into consciousness.
They come and go
Like the great expanse of clouds outside
My window,
Shifting and drizzling into
The vacuum of my endless night.

June 19, 2019 Oscar Jr.'s birthday

Dream

I dreamed about you on your birthday.
You wore that blue and black threadbare sweater
And smelled horridly of body odor and drugs.
I held your bulky self anyway.
I begged you to get help.
I begged you to let me help you.
You said
Maybe.

I went outside to drive our son to school
And there were police everywhere
Searching cars.
Our car was gone.
Impounded?
I knew they were coming for you next.

But you are dead, and out of reach.

I woke up weeping.

June 20, 2019

<u>Blood on the Hand</u>

I opened the door
Just enough
To let the little black puppy in.
I waited.
In a few minutes I heard the bed springs squeak
The TV grow louder.
Relief, he is still alive.

This morning when
He yelled at me
I saw dried blood
Around his arm and hand..
I gasped,
"OMG, the blood on your arm."
He looked
A shadow of shame
Crossed his face
Then became anger.
"Don't say that!"
Slamming back into his room.

Since, a few texts
Then silence
Stronger than the passing thunderstorm.

Two movies and a TV episode later
I sent in the dog.

He's alive another day.

June 30, 2019

July

It's the crape myrtle that
Flank me while I drive.
They started with the white,
Then the pink,
Then the magenta,
Now the lilac.
A gathering of sorts.

When I lived in Manhattan
Rachel was in a stroller.
I knew every street
That had tiny gardens.
I would weave us through the blocks,
North, then west, then north again
Until we got to her preschool.
It was amazing how many
Crocuses could fit into such small spaces.
I imagined city people on their knees
Desperate for greens
And yellows, covering cement with soil and hope.

First the crocus, then the daffodils, then the tulips.
The daffodils were my favorite.
The following September when she was four,
Confined to the hospital with a brain tumor,
I prayed for spring flowers
And for hope.

My prayers were answered.
I got my bulbs.
Thirty four years' worth
And Rachel blooms like a quaint perennial.
We move through different cities
Hundreds of miles apart.

I wonder about her flowers.
I wonder what accompanies on her daily trips
To Starbucks.

Woodstock

"We've got to get ourselves
Back to the garden" Joni Mitchell

We caravanned to Canada
On the Bicentennial.
The fresh waters of Lake Huron sparkled
Under the summer stars
As we drank Molson and smoked joints
On Ipperwash Beach.
Halfway between feminists and hippies,
We wore beads, fringe and ripped indigo denim.
Our lengthy hair drizzled down our backs
Auburn, blond, chestnut…
It was our version of Woodstock
Three days of peace and love
On the sands of the Canadian Great Lake.

I was wild for a woman
Whose sparkling eyes and amber hair
Chased my fears away.
But I might as well
Have tried to catch the wind.
As she had become distant.
I remember looking out
At the endless gentle waves
Lapping the shore,
Leaving tenuous teardrops on the bank.

Decades later I wonder what happened
To the wild woman who
Ruthlessly rushed into relationships
To relieve my worthlessness.

Today
The Great Lakes are thousands of miles away,
Woodstock is just a documentary
A clown is the president
But even worse,
Lovers are dead or gone
And my loneliness remains
Carved like a giant basin
By retreating weeping glaciers.

August 14, 2019

www.ingramcontent.com/pod-product-compliance
Ingram Content Group UK Ltd.
Pitfield, Milton Keynes, MK11 3LW, UK
UKHW041900190726
13854UKWH00003B/1002

9 780359 862610